THE
PLEASURES
OF

SUMMER
PICNICS

A Pavilion Companion

DEFINITION OF A PICNIC

Picnic: Originally a fashionable and social entertainment in which each person present contributed a share of the provisions; now, a pleasure party including an excursion to some spot in the country where all partake of a repast out of doors. . . . The essential feature was formerly the individual contribution; now it is the *al fresco* form of the repast.

Oxford English Dictionary

Bill of Fare for a Picnic
for 40 Persons

A joint of cold roast beef, a joint of cold boiled beef, 2 ribs of lamb, 2 shoulders of lamb, 4 roast fowls, 2 roast ducks, 1 ham, 1 tongue, 2 veal-and-ham pies, 2 pigeon pies, 6 medium-sized lobsters, 1 piece of collared calf's head, 18 lettuces, 6 baskets of salad, 6 cucumbers.

Stewed fruit well sweetened, and put into glass bottles well corked; 3 or 4 dozen plain pastry biscuits to eat with the stewed fruit, 2 dozen fruit turnovers, 4 dozen cheesecakes, 2 cold cabinet puddings in moulds, 2 blancmanges in moulds, a few jam puffs, 1 large cold plum-pudding (this must be good), a few baskets of fresh fruit, 3 dozen plain biscuits, a piece of cheese, 6 lbs. of butter (this, of course, includes the butter for tea), 4 quartern loaves of household bread, 3 dozen rolls, 6 loaves of tin bread (for tea), 2 plain plum cakes, 2 pound cakes, 2 sponge cakes, a tin of mixed biscuits, ½ lb. of tea. Coffee is not suitable for a picnic, being difficult to make.

Mrs Beeton's Book of Household Management, 1899

Planning the
Box Hill Picnic Excursion

Two or three more of the chosen only were to be admitted to join them, and it was to be done in a quiet, unpretending, elegant way, infinitely superior to the bustle and preparation, the regular eating and drinking, and picnic parade of the Eltons and the Sucklings.

It was now the middle of June, and the weather fine; and Mrs. Elton was growing impatient to name the day, and settle with Mr. Weston as to pigeon-pies and cold lamb, when a lame carriage-horse threw every thing into sad uncertainty. It might be weeks, it might be only a few days, before the horse were useable, but no preparations could be ventured on, and it was all melancholy stagnation. Mrs. Elton's resources were inadequate to such an attack.

Emma, Jane Austen, 1816

THE FREEDOM OF THE OPEN AIR

On Friday we sallied forth about twelve, – *we* comprehending Babbie, Mary and myself; with Gambardella for our only protector; and followed by Gambardella's maid carrying a basket of provisions, and a small Scotch terrier which kept us in perpetual excitement by biting our own and other people's heels. Having crossed the water to New Brighton in a Steamboat – a voyage in which even I could not manage to be sick – we were all set down on the beach to spend the day, and the prospect looked to me of the blackest! But before I had time to sink under it, Gambardella, with a sudden inspiration of genius, rushed off like a madman, and returned after a little while on the ugliest of created ponies, followed by two lads leading five donkeys to accommodate the whole party, maid and all: and on these creatures we actually rode eight miles, along the shore to a place called Leasowes and back again, sometimes galloping as if we had been on horseback, thanks to the lads, who shouted and belaboured us from behind, – and all the way in fits of laughter at the stupidity of the creatures and our own ridiculous appearance. At Leasowes we sent them to graze, and spread our provisions in a sand valley all covered with wild thyme and white roses. And Gambardella sang us Italian songs, and we ate sandwiches and drank a good deal of wine; – and *it was a good joy*!

Letter from Jane Welsh Carlyle to her husband Thomas, 1844

A SPIRITUAL PICNIC

The Spiritualists of New York and vicinity met lately on the grounds of Mr. Hoyt at Winfield, L.L. to participate in a pic-nic. At least, that was the ostensible object of the gathering, but the majority of the people, instead of desporting themselves on the green sward, formed a circle in a neighbouring thicket, and listened to the oral "manifestations." The assemblage did not exceed 200 persons, and most of the leading professors of "the science" were absent.

Our reporter then took a stroll through the thicket, and found a number of cozy little parties enjoying themselves in divers rational ways. A very interesting young lady, in golden ringlets, helped him to some excellent coffee and baked pears, for which he was very grateful. The lady and her sister, the daughters of the host, he was given to understand, were mediums of uncommon power.

Subsequently a circle was got up in another part of the thicket for the purpose of giving some physical manifestations to the reporters. But the old circle was speedily deserted for the new centre of attraction, and it grew proportionately large. A gentleman, whose wife was a medium, protested against joining hands in the circle, as it destroyed his wife's power as a medium. Exercises commence by singing:

"There is a land of pure delight."

Others sang in an entranced state; but their supernatural efforts were not very brilliant.

Excerpt from *The New York Times*, September 1857

THE DERBY DAY

A change of the moon in the previous week did not prophesy smooth things for the Epsom race goers. The weather, however, took a turn on the Tuesday evening, and the early dawn of the seventy-ninth Derby anniversary was only rather too sunny to inspire permanent hopes of its "staying a distance." . . . Carriages there were in plenty, full of veiled prophets to keep up the charter, but the dust was a mere trifle, and the crowds of stay-at-home Londoners who are content with Mr. Frith's transcript, and merely sauntered out into the thoroughfares at evening to watch them return, seemed quite disgusted at the very spruce appearance which those "noble sportsmen" maintained after the lockings and the lobsters, the chaff and the champagne, of the day, as they ran the gauntlet of their ironical cheers. The Duke of Malakoff came in among others for his share of comment, and the bearded warrior was the object of no little interest, as with his trio of Aides-de-Camp, he took his observations upon the indiscriminate lamb-and-chicken slaughter from his carriage on the hill.

Illustrated London News, May 22, 1858

TURFITES.

"I SAY, OLD FELLOW, HOW DO YOU GO TO THE DERBY THIS YEAR?"

"OH, THE OLD WAY—HAMPER AND FOUR."

QUEEN VICTORIA'S
HIGHLAND LUNCHEON

Cairn Lochan is a narrow valley, the river *Isla* winding through it like a silver ribbon, with trees at the bottom. The hills are green and steep, but towards the head of the valley there are fine precipices. We had then to take a somewhat circuitous route in order to avoid some bogs, and to come to a spot where we looked right up the valley for an immense distance; to the left, or rather more to the south, was *Glen Isla*, another glen, but wider, and not with the same high mountains as *Cairn Lochan*. Beyond *Glen Isla* were seen the *Lomond Hills* behind *Kinross*, at the foot of which is *Loch Leven*.

We sat on a very precipitous place, which made one dread any one moving backwards; and here, at a little before two o'clock, we lunched. The lights were charmingly soft, and, as I said before, like the bloom on a plum. The luncheon was very acceptable, for the air was extremely keen, and we found ice thicker than a shilling on the top of *Cairn Turc*, which did not melt when Brown took it and kept it in his hand.

Helena was so delighted, for this was *the only really great* expedition in which she had accompanied us.

Leaves from A Journal of Our Life in the Highlands Queen Victoria, 1868

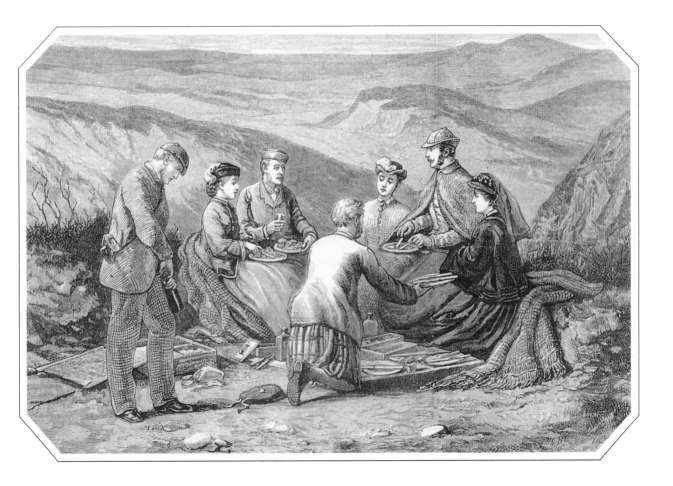

BREWING UP

It was extraordinary, he thought, how easily they adjusted to one another, and how little use she had for the flirtatious chitter-chatter that even working-class girls were beginning to cultivate, in imitation of the weekly magazine heroines. There was no restraint in her manner and no coyness either. He was just a man who paid her and her father for a job of work, and was therefore entitled to good service but no deference. In five minutes he had a fire going and in five more she had bread, bacon and eggs sizzling in a frying pan she had produced from somewhere. A tin kettle was filled and edged on to the improvised grate, and while she was busy he led the waggon under the trees, unbuckling the harness and turning the greys out to graze alongside the mare. She had, in that hamper of hers, everything necessary for a picnic – tin plates, enamel mugs, tea, a screw of salt, a couple of two-pronged forks, and even a phial of olive oil. "Dripping melts on the road," she said, "and the food tastes second-hand, no matter how hard you scour the pan. I like a fry-up now and again when I'm travelling, but more often I brew tea and live off bread and cheese."

God is An Englishman, R. F. Delderfield, 1970

A Fishing Picnic

VENATOR.   O my good master, this morning-walk has been spent to my great pleasure and wonder: but I pray, when shall I have your direction how to make artificial flies, like to those that the trout loves best, and also how to use them?

PISCATOR.   My honest scholar, it is now past five of the clock, we will fish till nine, and then go to breakfast. Go you to yon sycamore-tree and hide your bottle of drink under the hollow root of it; for about that time, and in that place, we will make a brave breakfast with a piece of powdered beef, and a radish or two that I have in my fish-bag; we shall, I warrant you, make a good honest, wholesome, hungry breakfast, and I will then give you direction for the making and using of your flies; and in the meantime there is your rod, and line, and my advice is, that you fish as you see me do, and let's try which can catch the first fish.

The Compleat Angler, Izaak Walton, 1653

BESIDE THE RIVER

22 JUNE 1870

The picnic party now came from the house to the landing stage and we saw them embark and push off. The boatman said the men were dissenting ministers and he laughed at them, calling them 'duck merchants'. I asked what he meant and he said it was a regular local name for these persons – because they were fond of ducks. They had a boat load of ducks on board now at any rate and they seemed to be having good fun for we heard the girls screaming and laughing across the water. Then they began to sing a rather pretty air. Another boat passed us with some students of Trevecca College rowing towards land. Meantime from the picnic party in the other boat came distant sounds of loud screaming and laughter as if a great romp were going on and as if the girls were being kissed and tickled.

Kilvert's Diary, Reverend Francis Kilvert, edited by William Plomer, 1930

Picnic on the Thames

A few strokes of the paddles sent the vessel away from the quay. 'A miss is as good as a mile replied the Yorkshireman. 'But pray what have you got in the hamper?'

'In the 'amper! Why, wittles to be sure. You seem to forget we are going a woyage, and 'ow keen the sea air is. I've brought a knuckle of weal, half a ham, beef, sarsingers, chickens, sherry white, and all that sort of thing, and werry acceptable they'll be by the time we get to the Nore, or may be before.

'*Ease her! Stop her!*' cried the captain through his trumpet, just as the vessel was getting into her stride in mid-stream, and, with true curiosity, the passengers flocked to the side, to see what was coming, though they could not possibly have examined half they had on board.

Jorrocks Jaunts and Jollities, R. S. Surtees, 1874

By the Sea

The horse was put up at a farm house and Martin ordered to beg borrow or (not steal, but) take some corn for him, and then bring up the luncheon hamper to the rocks. Martin appeared with the rug and basket and we had luncheon. He amused me by retiring to a respectful distance with his share of the provender and grinning over a rock, nothing but his black head to be seen, like a seal with a tall hat on. After luncheon we went down on the beach to look for sea anemones among the rocks and pools at low water for Mrs H. We found a green one. H. and I went out nearly to the end of the rocks where the waves were plunging and flying in foam over the reef, and presently we saw a large seal a hundred yards off fishing among the rocks near the shore. His black head was like a dog swimming and something like the head of a man. He dived suddenly, then came up again, disappeared again, and once more appeared with his large black shiny head not more than 50 yards from us, stationary, floating and riding easily, rising and falling with the swell, sometimes looking round at us with his great bright eye. It was the first seal I had ever seen wild, and I was delighted.

Grapes and claret on a grassy bank and we drove back to Camborne reaching Rosewarne at 7.

Kilvert's Diary, Reverend Francis Kilvert, edited by William Plomer, 1930

A VERY MERRY LUNCH OUTDOORS

"**T**ime for lunch," said Mr. Brooke, looking at his watch. "Commissary-general, will you make the fire and get water, while Miss March, Miss Sallie, and I spread the table? Who can make good coffee?"

"Jo can," said Meg, glad to recommend her sister. So Jo, feeling that her late lessons in cookery were to do her honour, went to preside over the coffee-pot, while the children collected dry sticks, and the boys made a fire, and got water from a spring near by. Miss Kate sketched, and Frank talked to Beth, who was making little mats of braided rushes to serve as plates.

The commander-in-chief and his aids soon spread the table-cloth with an inviting array of eatables and drinkables, prettily decorated with green leaves. Jo announced that the coffee was ready, and everyone settled themselves to a hearty meal; for youth is seldom dyspeptic, and exercise develops wholesome appetites. A very merry lunch it was; for everything seemed fresh and funny, and frequent peals of laughter startled a venerable horse who fed near by.

Little Women, Louisa M. Alcott, 1868

A Day in the Country

'It's ready,' said the serving girl, appearing in the doorway. They rushed off. But in the best spot, which Madame Dufour had already secretly picked out for them to sit at, two young men were already having their lunch. Quite likely they were the owners of the skiffs, for they were wearing rowing clothes.

They were stretched out in deck-chairs, almost lying down. Their faces were tanned dark brown by the sun and their torsos were covered by thin white cotton vests which left their arms bare, arms as muscular as a blacksmith's. They were strong and well-built and, though they put on the heartiness rather, every movement they made betrayed the supple grace of limb which comes with exercise and is a world away from the deforming effects on the working man of strenuous endlessly repeated labours.

They exchanged a quick smile when they saw the mother, and a look when they saw the girl! 'Let's let them have our place,' said one, 'it'll do for an introduction.'

The other got to his feet at once and, holding in his hand a cap which was half red and half black, he chivalrously offered the ladies the only spot in the garden where the sun was not beating down. The offer was accepted with profuse thanks; and to make the occasion more rustic, the family spurned tables and chairs and sat down on the grass.

The two young men moved their plates and glasses a few paces along and resumed eating. Their bare arms, which they displayed constantly, made the girl feel somewhat uncomfortable. She even made a point of turning her head away so as not to see them, while Madame Dufour, rather more boldly and stirred by a feminine curiosity which may have been desire, stared at them the whole time . . .

A Day in the Country, Guy de Maupassant, 1881, translated by David Coward, 1990

PASTORAL PICNIC

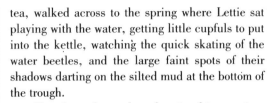

We wandered about picking flowers and talking until tea-time. A man-servant came with the tea-basket, and the girls spread the cloth under a great willow tree. Lettie took the little silver kettle, and went to fill it at the small spring which trickled into a stone trough all pretty with cranesbill and stellaria hanging over, while long blades of grass waved in the water. George, who had finished his work, and wanted to go home to

tea, walked across to the spring where Lettie sat playing with the water, getting little cupfuls to put into the kettle, watching the quick skating of the water beetles, and the large faint spots of their shadows darting on the silted mud at the bottom of the trough.

She glanced round on hearing him coming, and smiled nervously: they were mutually afraid of meeting each other again.

'It is about tea-time,' he said.

'Yes – it will be ready in a moment – this is not to make the tea with – it's only to keep a little supply of hot water.'

'Oh', he said, 'I'll go on home – I'd rather.'

'No,' she replied, 'you can't, because we are all having tea together: I had some fruits put up, because I know you don't trifle with tea – and your father's coming.'

'But,' he replied pettishly, 'I can't have my tea with all those folks – I don't want to – look at me!'

The White Peacock, D. H. Lawrence, 1911

Mrs Beeton's Picnic Luncheon

A more troublesome luncheon to provide is one for a picnic. We do not mean one of those grand ones where the same viands as would be found at an invitation lunch in a large establishment would be served with the same state and ceremony; but a delightfully informal meal perhaps got together at a day's notice where the different members of the party each make some contribution to the feast.

Now for this kind of meal it is not only essential that we have a menu, we also need a complete list of all articles required, independent of the actual food and drink.

A good deal of judgement is needed to plan out the different portions so that each person may take an equal part in providing; and for that reason it is better first, after making out the bill of fare, to reckon up the probable cost.

PICNIC LUNCHEON FOR 12 PERSONS

	s.	d.
Cold salmon (about 3 lbs.)...............	4	6
Mayonnaise sauce, cucumber (1 large)	1	3
Quarter of lamb, mint sauce..............	9	0
Chickens (2)	5	0
Tongue....................................	3	6
Salad, dressing	1	3
Fruit tarts (2).............................	2	0
Custard (1 qt.)	0	10
Jellies or creams (2).....................	3	0
Strawberries (2 qts.).....................	2	0
Cream (1 pt.).............................	1	6
½ lb. of cheese, 5d, ½ lb. of butter, 9d	1	2
2 loaves of bread.........................	0	6
1 lb. of biscuits	0	6
£1 16		0

Mrs Beeton's Book of Household Management, 1899

BOATING PICNIC

PICNICS.
TAKE THE MOTOR-BUS
FOR PICNICING.

When they had run and danced themselves dry, the girls quickly dressed and sat down to the fragrant tea. They sat on the northern side of the grove, in the yellow sunshine facing the slope of the grassy hill, alone in a little wild world of their own. The tea was hot and aromatic, there were delicious little sandwiches of cucumber and of caviare, and winy cakes.

'Are you happy, Prune?' cried Ursula in delight, looking at her sister.

'Ursula, I'm perfectly happy,' replied Gudrun gravely, looking at the westering sun.

'So am I.'

When they were together, doing the things they enjoyed, the two sisters were quite complete in a perfect world of their own. And this was one of the perfect moments of freedom and delight, such as children alone know, when all seems a *perfect* and blissful adventure.

When they had finished tea, the two girls sat on, silent and serene.

Women in Love, D. H. Lawrence, 1921

Opening up the Hamper

The Mole waggled his toes from sheer happiness, spread·his chest with a sigh of full contentment, and leaned back blissfully into the soft cushions. '*What* a day I'm having!' he said. 'Let us start at once!'

'Hold hard a minute, then!' said the Rat. He looped the painter through a ring in his landing-stage, climbed up into his hole above, and after a short interval reappeared staggering under a fat, wicker luncheon-basket.

'Shove that under your feet,' he observed to the Mole, as he passed it down into the boat. Then he untied the painter and took the sculls again.

'What's inside it?' asked the Mole, wriggling with curiosity.'

'There's cold chicken inside it,' replied the Rat briefly; 'coldtonguecoldhamcoldbeefpickledgherkinssaladfrenchrollscres-sandwigespottedmeatgingerbeerlemonadesodawater—'

'O stop, stop,' cried the Mole in ecstasies: 'This is too much!'

The Wind in the Willows, Kenneth Grahame, 1908

PACKING UP

"Well, well,' said the Rat. 'I suppose we ought to be moving. I wonder which of us had better pack the luncheon-basket?' He did not speak as if he was frightfully eager for the treat.

'O, please let me,' said the Mole. So, of course, the Rat let him.

Packing the basket was not quite such pleasant work as unpacking the basket. It never is. But the Mole was bent on enjoying everything, and although just when he had got the basket packed and strapped up tightly he saw a plate staring up at him from the grass, and when the job had been done again the Rat pointed out a fork which anybody ought to have seen, and last of all, behold! the mustard-pot, which he had been sitting on without knowing it – still, somehow, the thing got finished at last, without much loss of temper.

The afternoon sun was getting low as the Rat sculled gently homewards in a dreamy mood, murmuring poetry-things over to himself, and not paying much attention to Mole.

The Wind in the Willows, Kenneth Grahame, 1908

COLONIAL PICNIC

Our aides-de-camp gave a small fête champêtre yesterday in a valley called Annandale. The party, consisting of six ladies and six gentlemen, began at ten in the morning, and actually lasted till half-past nine at night. Annandale is a thick grove of fir-trees, which no sun can pierce. They had bows and arrows, a swing, battledore and shuttlecock, and a fiddle – the only fiddle in Simla; and they danced and eat all day, and seemed to have liked it throughout wonderfully. Oh dear! with my worn-out spirits and battered constitution, and the constant lassitude of India, it seems marvellous that any strength could stand that physical trial, but I suppose in our young Bromley ball days we should have thought it great fun. These young people did, at all events. They give another pic-nic next Thursday, and we are getting up some tableaux and charades which are to be acted here; the dining-room to be turned into a theatre. They are a very popular set of young men, and I bless their little hearts for taking so much trouble to carry on amusement; but I think they *go at it* rather too eagerly, and it will end in disappointment to some of them. The expense of these parties will not be so great to them, for both St. Cloup and Mars came to me yesterday to know what they were to do. 'Ces messieurs' had asked for a few 'petits plats', and a cook or two; and the man who makes ice had been to Mars for French fruits to make it with.

Up the Country, Emily Eden, 1866

Russian Picnic

The same three snipe flew over the sedge, their squeaks betraying alarm and vexation at being driven off the brook. The horses steadily munched and whinnied. Deniska attended them, trying to demonstrate his utter indifference to the cucumbers, pies and eggs that his masters were eating by plunging into the slaughter of the flies and horse-flies clinging to the animal's bellies and backs. Uttering a peculiar, venomously exultant guttural sound, he swatted his victims with gusto, grunting with annoyance when he missed and following each lucky fly that escaped death with his eyes.

'Deniska, what are you up to? Come and eat.' Kuzmichov sighed deeply – a sign that he was replete.

Deniska approached the mat diffidently and picked out five large yellow cucumbers – what they called 'yolkies' – not venturing to choose smaller, fresher specimens. He then took two black cracked hard-boiled eggs, and – hesitantly, as if afraid of someone slapping his outstretched hand – touched a pie with his finger.

'Go on, help yourself,' urged Kuzmichov.

Deniska seized the pie decisively, went off far to one side and sat on the ground, his back to the carriage. There ensued a chewing noise so loud that even the horses turned round and looked at Deniska suspiciously.

After his meal Kuzmichov got a bag containing something out of the carriage. 'I'm going to sleep,' he told Yegorushka. 'You mind no one takes this bag from under my head.'

The Steppe, Anton Chekhov, 1888,
translated by Ronald Hingley, 1965

No Mustard

To return to our present trip: nothing exciting happened, and we tugged steadily on to a little below Monkey Island, where we drew up and lunched. We tackled the cold beef for lunch, and then we found that we had forgotten to bring any mustard. I don't think I ever in my life, before or since, felt I wanted mustard as badly as I felt I wanted it then. I don't care for mustard as a rule, and it is very seldom that I take it at all, but I would have given worlds for it then.

I don't know how many worlds there may be in the universe, but anyone who had brought me a spoonful of mustard at that precise moment would have had them all. I grow reckless like that when I want a thing and can't get it.

Harris said he would have given worlds for mustard, too. It would have been a good thing for anybody who had come up to that spot with a can of mustard then; he would have been set up in worlds for the rest of his life.

Three Men in a Boat, Jerome K. Jerome, 1889

No Tin-opener

It cast a gloom over the boat, there being no mustard. We ate our beef in silence. Existence seemed hollow and uninteresting. We thought of the happy days of childhood, and sighed. We brightened up a bit, however, over the apple tart, and, when George drew out a tin of pine-apple from the bottom of the hamper, and rolled it in to the middle of the boat, we felt that life was worth living after all.

We are very fond of pine-apple, all three of us. We looked at the picture on the tin; we thought of the juice. We smiled at one another, and Harris got a spoon ready.

Then we looked for the knife to open the tin with. We turned out everything in the hamper. We turned out the bags. We pulled up the boards at the bottom of the boat. We took everything out on to the bank and shook it. There was no tin-opener to be found.

Then Harris tried to open the tin with a pocket-knife, and broke the knife and cut himself badly; and George tried a pair of scissors, and the scissors flew up, and nearly put his eye out. While they were dressing their wounds, I tried to make a hole in the thing with the spikey end of the hitcher, and the hitcher slipped and jerked me out between the boat and the bank into two feet of muddy water, and the tin rolled over, uninjured, and broke a teacup.

Then we all got mad. We took that tin out on the bank, and Harris went up into a field and got a big sharp stone, and I went back into the boat and brought out the mast, and George held the tin and Harris held the sharp end of his stone against the top of it and I took the mast and poised it high up in the air and gathered up all my strength and brought it down.

It was George's straw hat that saved his life that day. He keeps that hat now (what is left of it).

Three Men in a Boat, Jerome K. Jerome, 1889

They saw the robin carry food to his mate two or three times and it was so suggestive of afternoon tea that Colin felt they must have some.

"Go and make one of the menservants bring some in a basket to the rhododendron walk," he said. "And then you and Dickon can bring it here."

It was an agreeable idea; easily carried out, and when the white cloth was spread upon the grass, with hot tea and buttered toast and crumpets, a delightfully hungry meal was eaten, and several birds on domestic errands paused to inquire what was going on and were led into investigating crumbs with great activity. Nut and Shell whisked up trees with pieces of cake and Soot took the entire half of a buttered crumpet into a corner and pecked at and examined and turned it over and made hoarse remarks about it until he decided to swallow it all joyfully in one gulp.

The afternoon was dragging towards its mellow hour. The sun was deepening the gold of its lances, the bees were going home and the birds were flying past less often. Dickon and Mary were sitting on the grass, the tea-basket was repacked ready to be taken back to the house, and Colin was lying against his cushions with his heavy locks pushed back from his forehead and his face looking quite a natural colour.

The Secret Garden, Frances Hodgson Burnett, 1911

About Picnics

To-day I am going to write about picnics, because I look on them as so essential and delightful a part of our English life, that they cannot be omitted from any chronicle of meals.

I myself love a picnic of all things, and consider that food tastes twice as nice when eaten *al fresco*. My husband, unfortunately, feels quite the opposite. To begin with, he has a childish dislike – I would almost say fear if I didn't know him to be a soldier and a brave gentleman – of wasps. And though I have made for all my friends pretty and useful little brooches in the form of bunches of grapes, the fruit being made of tiny blue bags in case of bee stings, and the leaves of tinted lumps of soda for wasp stings, Addle utterly refuses to wear one and simply flaps *The Times* (which he insists on taking on a picnic, thereby, to my mind, completely ruining the idyllic spirit) at the wasps, which only seems to encourage them. 'Really, my dear boy,' I said to him once, 'you're behaving like a child of two.' 'I wish I were a child of two,' he replied. 'Then I wouldn't have been allowed to come at all.'

Lady Addle at Home, Mary Dunn, 1945

TALE OF THE BEEFSTEAK PIE

You see, it was in this way: we were sitting in a meadow, about ten yards from the water's edge, and we had just settled down comfortably to feed. Harris had the beefsteak pie between his knees, and was carving it, and George and I were waiting with our plates ready.

"Have you got a spoon there?" says Harris; "I want a spoon to help the gravy with."

The hamper was close behind us, and George and I both turned round to reach one out. We were not five seconds getting it. When we looked round again, Harris and the pie were gone! . . .

George and I gazed all about. Then we gazed at each other. "Has he been snatched up to heaven?" I queried.

"They'd hardly have taken the pie, too," said George.

With a sigh, we turned our eyes once more towards the spot where Harris and the pie had last been seen on earth; and there, as our blood froze in our veins and our hair stood up on end, we saw Harris's head – and nothing but his head – sticking bolt upright among the tall grass, the face very red, and bearing upon it an expression of great indignation!

George was the first to recover.

"Speak!" he cried, "and tell us whether you are alive or dead – and where is the rest of you?"

"Oh, don't be a stupid ass!" said Harris's head, "I believe you did it on purpose."

"Did what?" exclaimed George and I.

"Why, put me to sit here – darn silly trick! Here, catch hold of the pie."

And out of the middle of the earth, as it seemed to us, rose the pie – very much mixed up and damaged; and after it scrambled Harris – tumbled, grubby and wet.

He had been sitting, without knowing it, on the very verge of a small gully, the long grass hiding it from view; and in leaning a little back he had shot over, pie and all.

Three Men in a Boat, Jerome K. Jerome, 1889

HOLIDAY MEMORY

This was the morning when father, mending one hole in the thermos-flask, made three; when the sun declared war on the butter, and the butter ran; when dogs, with all the sweet-binned backyards to wag and sniff and bicker in, chased their tails in the jostling kitchen, worried sand-shoes, snapped at flies, writhed between legs, scratched among towels, sat smiling on hampers.

And if you could have listened at some of the open doors of some of the houses in the street you might have heard:

'Uncle Owen says he can't find the bottle-opener . . .'
'Has he looked under the hallstand?'
'Willy's cut his finger . . .'
'Got your spade?'
'If somebody doesn't kill that dog . . .'
'Uncle Owen says why should the bottle-opener be under the hallstand?'
'Never again, never again . . .'
'I know I put the pepper somewhere . . .'
'Willy's bleeding . . .'
'Look, there's a bootlace in my bucket . . .'
'Oh come *on*, come on . . .'
'Let's have a look at the bootlace in your bucket . . .'
'If I lay my hands on that dog . . .'
'Uncle Owen's found the bottle-opener . . .'
'Willy's bleeding over the cheese . . .'

And the trams that hissed like ganders took us all to the beautiful beach.

Quite Early One Morning, Dylan Thomas, 1954

ACKNOWLEDGEMENTS

PICTURE CREDITS

Front cover: *A Toast to the Bugler*, Christopher Monies (Bridgeman Art Library/Josef Mensing Gallery, Hamm-Rhynern)
Title page: *A Riverside Picnic*, Harold Piffard (Fine Art Photographs)

3 *Easter Monday at Brooklands, 1923* (Hulton Picture Company)
5 *An Alpine Fete*, Casimiro Radice (Bridgeman Art Library)
6 (Punch)
7 *A Toast to the Bugler*, Christopher Monies (Bridgeman Art Libraries)
9 *View over London from Hampstead Heath*, John Ritchie (Bridgeman/Fine Art Society, London)
11 *The Picnic*, Valentine Cameron Prinsep (Bridgeman/Forbes Magazine Collection, New York)
13 *The Derby Day*, William Powell Frith (Tate Gallery, London)
14 (Mary Evans Picture Library)
15 *The Queen, Prince Consort and Royal Family at Luncheon at Cairn Lochan* (Mansell Collection)
16 (Punch)
17 *The Picnic*, Charles Robert Leslie (Fine Art Photographs)
19 *The Picnic*, H. Verron-Favre (Fine Art Photographs/Gavin Graham Gallery)
20 (Mary Evans Picture Library)
21 *Our Picnic, New Lock, Berks*, Charles James Lewis (Bridgeman/Christopher Wood Gallery)
22 (Punch)
23 *The Thames*, James Tissot (Wakefield Art Gallery and Museum)
25 *A Picnic on the Coast, Isle of Wight*, James Whaite (Bridgeman/Bonhams)
26 *Tea Out of Doors* (Hulton Picture Company)
27 *The Picnic*, James Tissot (Bridgeman/Musée des Beaux Arts, Dijon)

29 *The Picnic*, Claude Monet (Scala/Pushkin Museum, Moscow)
30 (Mary Evans Picture Library)
31 *Holyday*, James Tissot (Tate Gallery, London)
33 *Picnic in 1869* (Hulton Picture Company)
34 (Mary Evans Picture Library)
35 *The Riverside Picnic*, Edward Ridley (Fine Art Photographers)
36 *Mole and Ratty picnicking*, Arthur Rackham (Mary Evans Picture Library)
37 *A Scotch Picnic, 1921* (Hulton Picture Company)
39 *An Interrupted Picnic*, Charles Sims (Bridgeman)
41 *The Picnic*, Colonel E. A. P. Hobday (National Army Museum)
43 *Picnic In the Open Air*, Nikolij Sokolov (Scala/State Gallery Tretyakov, Moscow)
45 *Men Having a Picnic, 1900* (Hulton Picture Company)
47 *Henley, July 1914* (Hulton Picture Company)
49 *The Picnic*, James Charles (Bridgeman/Warrington Museum and Art Gallery, Lancs)
50 (Mary Evans Picture Library)
51 *Army Point to Point, 1924* (Popperfoto)
53 *Newmarket and Thurlow Point to Point, Suffolk 1935* (Hulton Picture Company)
54 (Punch)
55 *In the Sunshine*, Frans Gaillard (Bridgeman/Whitford and Hughes, London)

TEXT CREDITS

Text extracts from the following sources are reprinted with the kind
permission of the publishers and copyright holders stated. Should any
copyright holder have been inadvertently omitted they should apply to
the publishers who will be pleased to credit them in any subsequent
editions.

16 R. F. Delderfield, *God Is an Englishman* (Hodder & Stoughton,
1970/David Higham Associations)

28 Guy de Maupassant, *A Day In the Country and Other Stories* (translated
by David Coward, World's Classics paperback 1990, reprinted by
permission of Oxford University Press)

30 D. H. Lawrence, *The White Peacock* (copyright © 1983 by the Estate of
Frieda Lawrence Ravagli. Used by permission of Viking Penguin, a
division of Penguin Books USA Inc.)

34 D. H. Lawrence, *Women in Love* (copyright 1920, 1922 by D. H.
Lawrence, renewed 1948, 1950 by Frieda Lawrence. Used by
permission of Viking Penguin, a division of Penguin Books USA Inc.)

42 Anton Chekhov, *The Steppe and Other Stories* (translated by Ronald
Hingley, World's Classics paperback 1991, reprinted by permission of
Oxford University Press)

44 Mary Dunn, *Lady Addle at Home* (Methuen 1945)

54 Dylan Thomas, *Quite Early One Morning* (J. M. Dent © Dylan Thomas
1954)

First published in Great Britain 1992 by
PAVILION BOOKS LIMITED
196 Shaftesbury Avenue, London WC2H 8JL

Anthology compilation copyright © Jenny de Gex 1992
For other copyright holders see Acknowledgements.

Designed by Andrew Barron & Collis Clements Associates

A CIP catalogue record for this book is available
from the British Library

ISBN 1-85145-800-X

Printed and bound in Scotland by Eagle Colour Books